Tab in a Cap!

By Debbie Croft

I am Pam.

I can see a pet cat.

The cat sits at a mat in a hat.

Tab is my pet cat.

See the cap, Tab?

Tab can see the cap.

I can sit at the mat.

Tab can sit at the mat
in my cap!

Sit, Tab, sit!

Tab sits at the mat in my cap.

CHECKING FOR MEANING

1. Where does Tab sit in the story? *(Literal)*

2. What does Pam have that Tab can put on? *(Literal)*

3. Why do you think Tab wears a cap? *(Inferential)*

EXTENDING VOCABULARY

pet	Look at the word *pet*. What sounds are in this word? Which sound is changed to turn *pet* into *bet*?
sits	Look at the word *sits*. What is the base of this word? What has been added to the base?
cap	Look at the word *cap*. Can you think of another word that means the same as *cap*?

MOVING BEYOND THE TEXT

1. How do you think Tab feels when wearing the cap? How do you know?

2. Why do you think some people like dressing up their pets? Do you think the pets like it?

3. Do animals normally wear clothes?

4. What else might a cat wear?

SPEED SOUNDS

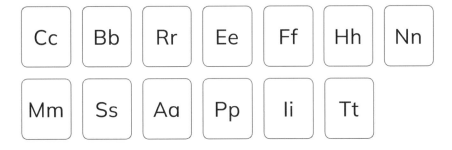

| Cc | Bb | Rr | Ee | Ff | Hh | Nn |

| Mm | Ss | Aa | Pp | Ii | Tt |

PRACTICE WORDS

pet

can

hat

cat

in

cap

Tab